Target Grammar

Book 1

Contents

NOUNS 4

ONE AND MANY 9

COUNTABLE AND UNCOUNTABLE NOUNS 12

GENDERS 15

THIS AND THAT 19

A, AN AND THE 23

VERBS 25

OPPOSITES 29

DESCRIBING THINGS 32

HE AND SHE 37

PUNCTUATION 39

FULL STOP 41

SENTENCES 42

WHERE ARE THEY? 43

LET'S REVISE 45

Note for Parents and Teachers

We speak our mother tongue even before we realise it. As for grammar, we're not even conscious of this aspect of language at that time. Later, however, it is the practice of grammar that helps us perfect our ability with a language.

While the most commonly understood meaning of the word 'grammar' is 'rules of a language', it would be better to say that the grammar of a language comprises all the aspects of a language which, when learnt, improves our communication— both spoken and written.

Today, the teaching of English grammar is encouraged more than ever. This series called **Target Grammar**, is a carefully graded series of 5 books covering all the basic items of English grammar. These books can be used at home or in the classroom as a part of the school curriculum. A key feature of this series is that the books have been written in such a manner that children can use them by themselves, without a teacher or any other help.

These books provide a good understanding of the English language and are replete with examples and exercises which assist greatly in the learning of grammar by young children.

NOUNS

Nouns are naming words that we use to name things. In other words they are the names of animals, people, things or places.

Nouns are basically of two types— **Proper nouns and Common nouns**.

Proper nouns are the names of some particular places, people or objects. They always begin with capital letters.

Bible

Paris

Anna

Mr Brown

Common nouns are the names of all the things that we commonly see around us. They never begin with capital letters.

1. The given list shows a few common and proper nouns. Can you think of at least 5 more nouns for each column and write them down?

People	Place	Animal	Thing
policeman	market	bird	sandwich
baker	beach	tiger	bicycle
Dr Sim	museum	cow	almirah
queen	Tower Bridge	Anaconda	fan
....	....	....	....
....	....	....	....
....	....	....	....
....	....	....	....
....	....	....	....

2. Look at the picture carefully. List the nouns that you see and write them in the space provided.

3. Given below is a list of nouns. Look around and see how many of them can you find? Tick those which you see.

☐	window	☐	teacher
☐	door	☐	staircase
☐	table	☐	brother
☐	chair	☐	sister
☐	cat	☐	cloud
☐	bus	☐	cycle
☐	flower	☐	pencil
☐	telephone		

ONE AND MANY

When we find something that is more than one, we form plurals.

Most nouns form their plurals by adding either 's' or 'es' at the end of the noun.

ball – balls

cat – cats

fox – foxes

If a noun ends in 'y', then the 'y' changes into 'i' and 'es' is added at the end of the word.

baby – babies

fairy – fairies

jelly – jellies

If a noun ends in 'y' with a vowel before it, add only 's' to form plurals.

monkey – monkeys

key – keys

day – days

If a noun ends with 'f' or 'fe', then you simply change the 'f' or 'fe' to 'v' and add 'es' to form their plural.

leaf - lea**ves**

knife – kni**ves**

wolf – wol**ves**

 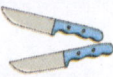  

Some nouns have the same spelling for the singular and the plural forms. For such nouns we use numbers to denote plurals.

one sheep, **two** sheep

one deer, **two** deer

Some nouns are used only in their plural form.

Scissors

pants

clothes

Sometimes the letter or letters within the nouns are changed a little to form their plurals.

woman – women

  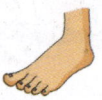 

mouse – mice

foot – feet

Complete the table given below. A few have been done for you.

Singular	Plural	Singular	Plural
hat	hats	wife	wives
lady	....	....	candies
box	....	....	lamps
ice cream	....	....	classes
bus	....	....	eyes
shoe	....	....	watches
cow	....	....	knives
bag	....	....	books
penny	....	....	fans
cake	....	....	pencils
leaf	....	....	mice
taxi	....	....	feet
army	....	....	sheep

COUNTABLE AND UNCOUNTABLE NOUNS

Countable nouns are those which can be counted like books, girls, bikes and cars. For such nouns we ask **how many?**

Uncountable nouns are those which cannot be counted like sugar, hair and water. For such nouns we ask **how much?**

Countable nouns are either singular or plural. We use **is** when we talk of singular nouns and **are** when we talk of plural nouns.

Our cat **is** playing.

Our cats **are** playing.

1. Pick out the countable and uncountable nouns and write them in their correct columns.

food

bear

bell

cola

rain

wind

Countable nouns	Uncountable nouns

2. Fill in the blanks with 'much' and 'many'.

How .... rice did you eat yesterday?

Richard bought .... kites.

Dorothy picked .... flowers for her teacher.

How .... sugar will you take in your tea?

GENDERS

Genders are words which tell us whether a noun is a man or a woman. If a noun is a man, it belongs to the masculine gender. If it is a woman, it belongs to the feminine gender.

Sometimes different words are used for masculine and feminine genders.

Masculine **Feminine**

boy

girl

uncle

aunt

husband											wife

father											mother

Sometimes the form of the word changes while changing the gender.

Masculine					**Feminine**

actor											actress

lion											lioness

shepherd　　　　　　　　　　　shepherdess

When we use the masculine gender, we use he. When we use the feminine gender, we use she.

David is a football player. He plays very well.

Jenny is a teacher. She teaches Maths.

Can you put the given nouns in the right columns?

bride

grandmother

prince

nephew

queen

sister

cow

grandson

Masculine	Feminine

THIS AND THAT

This is used when you want to show something lying near you.

This is my book.

This is my mother.

This is Jane's car.

This is Jacob's dog.

That is used to show things that are far away from us.

That is an apple tree.

That is my school.

That is my home.

That is an aeroplane.

This is my teacher and that is my friend.

This is a cat and that is a lion.

This is a pen and that is a truck.

Make 2 sentences using **this** and **that** at the same time. One has been done for you.

This is a cake and that is my sister.

A, AN AND THE

When we talk of some single noun we use a or an before it.

If the noun begins with a vowel sound (a, e, i, o, u) then an is used before them.

When we talk of something in particular we use the.

the moon

the sun

the pole star

Fill in the blanks with **a, an** or **the**.

Rita ate .... apple.

Mom bought .... bat and .... umbrella.

Yesterday I ate .... ice cream.

Dad bought .... teddy bear, ... toy car and .... aeroplane for me.

Sun rises in .... east.

VERBS

Words which tell us about some work are called doing words or Verbs.

Tony sings in the choir.

Alice walks to school.

Mother cooks pasta everyday.

1. Fill in the blanks with the words in the help box. One has been done for you.

| jump   sing   bring   catch   eat   fly   tell   drive |

a. I can jump high.

b. Can you .... a ball?

c. '.................... your lunch quickly or it will turn cold,' said mom.

d. Planes .... high up in the sky.

e. 'Can you .... me the answer?' asked the teacher.

f. Tomorrow we will .... to our grandmother's house.

g. The girls will .... at the party.

h. '.................... me the hammer,' said dad.

2. Different animals can do different things. Choose the correct verbs and fill in the blanks below.

| barks | perching | purr | swing | swim |

a. A dog ....

b. Monkeys can .... from branch to branch.

c. In the river the fishes ....

d. Cats .... when they are happy.

e. Can you see the bird .... ?

3. Colour the verbs used in this short story.

Mimi lay in bed. 'I do not feel well,' she told her father. Her father put his hand on her head. 'You are very hot,' he said. 'I think you have fever. You will have to stay at home from school today.'

Mimi's father went to the kitchen. He brought Mimi a glass of water. Then he made a phone call to tell Mimi's friend that she would not go to school with her that day. Poor Mimi spent two whole days in bed. Sometimes she read, sometimes she slept. Her parents cared for her and soon she was well again.

OPPOSITES

Opposites are words which mean the opposite of another word.

fast

slow

thin

thick

inside

outside

1. Match the word with their correct opposites.

A	B
big	soft
fast	tall
cold	outside
sad	slow
short	old
inside	thick
right	hot
hard	left
thin	small
young	happy

2. **Write the opposite words for the given words. The first one has been done for you.**

clean	dirty
good	....
here	....
out	....
soft	....
many	....
hot	....
wide	....
sweet	....
strong	....
happy	....
long	....
rich	....

DESCRIBING THINGS

red flower

fat man

tall tree

happy child

The red coloured words here are all describing words or adjectives because they tell you more about the nouns.

Look at the sentences below and note the words in red. All these words are describing words.

The garden is colourful and lovely. It is full of red, yellow, blue and pink flowers. There are tall trees here. The trees are green.

1. Give a describing word for each noun or naming word given below. Two have been done for you.

| blue sky | | tall tree |

.... boy

.... tea

.... hair

.... blackboard

.... wall

.... shoes

.... clouds

.... knife

.... grass

2. Use a colour pencil to underline the adjectives used in this short story.

The little boy in the striped shirt and brown shorts looked out of the big window. The grey sky was covered with black clouds. Every now and then he could see bright lightening and hear the booming of thunder. Big drops of rain began to fall on the dark street, on the green leaves of the trees in the small garden and on the colourful clothes that were hanging on the clothesline. He was glad to be inside. His room was warm and he had lots of exciting books to read.

3. Match the adjectives with the animals they describe.

Adjective	Noun

white	tiger

grey	polar bear

long	monkey

striped	elephant

noisy	snake

HE AND SHE

Often we use he or she instead of a person's name. If it is a boy or a man, we use he. And if we talk of a girl or a lady we use she. Such words which are used instead of nouns are called **Pronouns.**

Alfred is a good boy. He paints beautiful pictures.

Rosy is my sister. She likes to swim.

When we talk of animals and non living things, we often refer to them as **it**.

This is my dog. **It** is called Cupid.

This is the teacher's desk. **It** is big.

1. Fill in the spaces with he, she or it. The first one has been done for you.

a. John can fly a kite. <u>He</u> can fly it.

b. The girl stayed in bed. .... was unwell.

c. Have you seen the cat anywhere? Have you seen .... ?

d. The man was trying to catch the bus. .... was running.

e. Carla's mother made a beautiful garden. .... takes care of the plants herself.

f. The boy was late home from school. .... was busy playing basketball.

PUNCTUATION

Look at the letters below. They are called Capital letters.

A B C D E F G H I J K L M N O
P Q R S T U V W X Y Z

> Capital letters are used for the first letter of all proper nouns such as the names of people, places, days of the week, months of the year. We also use capital letters when we begin a sentence.

America

Orchard Road

Angela

Tuesday

River Thames

David

John Smith

February

Write your own name ....

Write your best friend's name ....

Circle the letters of the given words that should be in capital letters.

worm

rhine river

road

africa

october

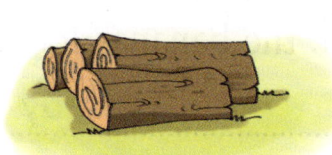
wood

peter

street

waterfall

tuesday

FULL STOP

Whenever we complete a sentence we put a **full stop** at the end.

Richard and I played in the rain.

We live in Frankfurt.

Add full stops and capital letters to the sentences given below.

a. the bananas looked ripe

....

b. the children bought sweets

....

c. amy likes to eat apples

....

d. i love to play in the rain

....

e. mom gave me a gift

....

SENTENCES

Sentences are groups of words that have a complete meaning.

Angela is wearing a pink dress.

Can you arrange the words in order to make proper sentences? The first one has been done for you. Don't forget the full stops at the end of each sentence.

a. boy the balloon carried red a

   The boy carried a red balloon.
....

b. ice creams the ate children

....

c. dancing girls were the singing and

....

d. jane bicycle a bought new

....

e. school they late for are

....

WHERE ARE THEY?

Preposition are words which show the relationship between a noun or a pronoun with the rest of the sentence.

The cottage was beside the waterfall.

Jenny is standing behind Ruth.

The cat sat on the mat.

The child is under the table.

He held the umbrella over his head.

Peter ran across the road.

1. Underline the prepositions given in the sentences.

a. The mouse is under the table.

b. The wind blew across the field.

c. She is at the party.

d. We are in the shop.

e. The children ran around the playground.

f. The waves ran over the sand.

2. Now make up your own sentences using the prepositions given below.

      below   behind   near

a. ....

....

b. ....

....

c. ....

....

LET'S REVISE

1. Put the given words into the correct columns.

water   Japan   Saturday   football   soldier   dress

Proper noun	Common noun

2. Put the following nouns into the correct columns.

eggs   bowls   time   milk   chocolate   spoon
happiness   smile   sleep   food   tent   noise

Countable nouns   **Uncountable nouns**

3. Put the following words into the correct columns

| bike   plane   eagle   ice cream   uncle   shoe afternoon   apple   cave   envelope |

a	an
....	....
....	....
....	....
....	....
....	....
....	....

4. Circle the verbs in the given passage.

It was a sunny morning. Alia got up and looked out of her window. She brushed her teeth and took a bath. Then she ate her breakfast. At 8o'clock, Alia walked to school. Her pet cat Sammy ran behind her. Meaow! Meaow! It called out loudly to her.

5. Write down the opposite of the given words.

poor–....................

thick–....................

cloudy–....................

loud–....................

wide–....................

uncle–....................

tall–....................

6. Circle the adjectives in the sentences.

                         The tall giraffe ate leaves.

Pam sold her red sweater.

                               I bought red balloons.

          My teacher had long hair.

7. Write down the correct pronoun for the given words.

Nouns	Pronouns
dog	
actress	
grandfather	
tree	
sister	

8. Rewrite the sentences using capital letters where necessary.

yesterday alec fell from his cycle.

....

greece is a beautiful country.

....

lion is the king of the jungle.

....

my friend della likes the blue colour.

....

jim, clara and fiona went to play in the park.

....

9. Tick the correct preposition in the given sentences.

She walked on/under the bridge.

Diana stood behind/above the door.

The strawberries are in/below the basket.

Potatoes and onions grow under/over the ground.

10. Arrange the groups of jumbled words into sentences. Remember to finish the sentences with a full stop.

cat on tree the is the

....

I to football love play

....